THE MILLER AND HIS MEN:

A MELO-DRAME,

In Two Acts,

BY I. POCOCK ESQ.

Author of John of Paris, The Magpie or the Maid, Robinson Crusoe, &c.

PRINTED FROM THE ACTING COPY, WITH REMARKS,
BIOGRAPHICAL AND CRITICAL, BY D—G.

To which are added,

A DESCRIPTION OF THE COSTUME,—CAST OF THE CHARACTERS,
ENTRANCES AND EXITS,—RELATIVE POSITIONS OF THE PER-
FORMERS ON THE STAGE,—AND THE WHOLE OF THE STAGE
BUSINESS.

As performed at the

THEATRES ROYAL, LONDON.

EMBELLISHED WITH A FINE ENGRAVING,
By MR. BONNER, from a Drawing taken in the Theatre, by
MR. R. CRUIKSHANK.

LONDON:

JOHN CUMBERLAND, 6, BRECKNOCK PLACE,
CAMDEN NEW TOWN.

REMARKS.

The Miller and his Men.

THE art of *war*—and, no less, the *dramatic art*, have been greatly advanced by the invention of *gunpowder*. The battles of antiquity were fought "lance to lance, and horse to horse;" and unless a man could do the execution of Richard—

> "Methinks there be six Richmonds in the field,—
> *Five* have I slain to-day, instead of him!"

or enact the prowess of Bobadil—" Twenty more; kill *them!*" armies might be whole days hacking and hewing each other before either side was finally exterminated. Besides your less ardent and more discreet warrior, who has adopted the better part of valour, might feel his courage oozing out at his fingers' ends when engaged in close quarters; but a long shot relieves him from the immediate presence of his enemy, gives him time to recruit his spirits, and the work of havoc goes bravely on, from this distant, and consequently more polite, mode of warfare. To the *drama*, gunpowder has proved an invaluable auxiliary—*Shakspeare* and the *German Monk* may fairly divide the crown. When

language fails, and invention is at a stand, what fills up
the awkward interval with such effect as a flash—(O
for a muse of *fire !*") not of *wit*, but of gunpowder ?—A
piece with an explosion is sure to go off well ; and
many an author can bear grateful testimony that, when
deserted by genius, he has been saved by, gunpowder.

The plot of the Miller and his Men is unusually com-
bustible.—Claudine, a young Bohemian lass, is ad-
dressed by two lovers of very opposite characters :
Lothair, a fellow of exceeding honesty, but miserably
poor ; and Grindoff, the miller, a rogue in grain, with
money in his purse. The father of Claudine would
have Grindoff for his son-in-law ; his daughter is all for
love, and the miller well lost, and prefers Lothair. It
chances, that while the latter is passing through a neigh-
bouring forest, he hears some banditti pronounce the
name of Claudine ; this bodes no good : he acquaints
her father with the circumstance ; volunteers a crusade
against the robbers—should he fall, let Claudine be the
bride of Grindoff; but if he return alive and merry, let
his desert in arms be crowned in those of the fair vil-
lager. Old Kelmar consents—a storm, exceedingly
well got up, now begets an awful attention in the audi-
ence, in the midst of which, two travellers, Count Frederick Friberg, and his attendant, Karl, lost in a labyrinth, without love or liquor, lay our risible faculties
under contribution. They arrive at Kelmar's cottage.—
Friberg recognises in his ancient host the *once* richest

tenant of his late father's land ; he inquires what has thus reduced him to poverty and a hovel—'twill chill their hearts to hear—Karl, at this intelligence, earnestly begs that he will spare them the relation, their bodies being already cramped with *cold*. Karl is indeed any. thing but a philosopher ; his complaints, however, are amusing—head broke, body bruised, joints dislocated, not three square inches about him unscarified with briers and brambles—no food, hourly expectation of the wolves making a meal of him, and, that he might sup full with horrors, two polite gentlemen, with long knives, paying their respects to him. The Miller was conversing with Kelmar when the travellers entered ; the Count, who has some faint remembrance of his features, eyes him with a keen glance, from which Grindoff turns away. His sable physiognomy makes no very favourable impression on Karl, who (as Foote said of Macklin), thinks, if God writes a legible hand, that man must be a villain. Grindoff had been an attentive listener to Karl's story of his adventures ; but when he comes to the banditti business, and produces a poniard, which the rogues in their confusion left behind, he makes an effort to obtain it, but is foiled in the attempt. Taking advantage of the Miller's absence, Kelmar enters a little into his biography—this brings to the Count's re- collection a favoured servant of his father's, one *Wolf*, a villain who betrayed his trust, and, by taxing his memory still further, he is convinced that Mr. Wolf, like other rogues, has added an *alias* to his name. It is *conveniently* arranged that the Miller shall drop his scabbard, that Karl shall pick it up, and that it shall exactly fit the dagger which the banditti left behind. Alarm seizes both master and man—they are snared— Kelmar and his daughter are surely in the plot: they are about to retreat, when their evil spirit, Grindoff, re-appears. To travel *instanter* is impossible : the torrent has swept the ferry-barge from the shore and driven it down the stream; the night is dark ; and robbers are a foot. They are crows' meat, to a certainty ! It is now full time to return to Lothair, who, in disguise, en-counters the banditti in the forest, offers to join them, and is admitted to that honourable fraternity, after gag-ging them with a fictitious tale about his having been in the service of Count Friberg, but, being disgraced for " *no good*," like the brace of sinners ordered to our lady's shrine—

" Which at Loretto dwelt, in wax, stone, wood,
    And in a fair white wig look'd wondrous fine"—

he had absconded from punishment, to seek " the at-tribute of Gods," revenge. He is led blindfolded to the robber's cavern, where he contemplates a scene of un-lawful jollification, that only finds its parallel in *Gil Blas*. In this den there is a recess, over which is posted this inflammatory placard, " *Powder Magazine.*" Ra-vina, the *ci-devant* mistress of the robber chief, who, as may be reasonably anticipated, is Grindoff, now enters, and gives a tragic tone to the scene. She has endured seven years' captivity, and is now about to be discarded for a new flame of the miller's. The *green-eyed* monster, instead of the *black*, wholly possesses her, and Ravina, by an easy transition, rises from a harlot into a heroine. Grindoff, on his entrance into the cave, starts at the sight of a stranger, but Lothair is so well disguised, that he does not recognise him. A council of war is now held, and the destruction of Friberg is determined on. Lothair offers to be the assassin—this favour is denied: but, after some parley, he is permitted to join the miller, and Riber, a brother butcher, in this hopeful enterprise.

The Count and Karl, after all their dangers, are quietly reposing in Kelmar's cottage, when Riber enters, followed by Grindoff. The former is to pistol the Count, the latter is to steal Claudine and bear her off, *a la Pluto and Proserpine,* to the cavern. The slumbers of Karl had been grievously disturbed by visionary rats; he awakes, observes Riber, watches his motions, and, as the villain is in the act of levelling his pistol at the Count, grasps his dagger, and stabs him to the heart. This produces a stirring scene of melodramatic confusion, which those who know the effect of dark lanterns, shrieks, and pistol-shots, can readily conceive.

Behold Claudine, in the cavern, recognised by her lover, Lothair, and about to be poisoned by the jealous Ravina. But curiosity chides our dull delay; we must haste to the *powder magazine,* and exhibit Lothair pointing out the *train* to Ravina, explaining his intention, presenting her with a phosphorous-bottle, and instructing her how to do the needful. She declines the honour; when Lothair himself sets fire to the train, and a most satisfactory explosion takes place.

The piece was got up with splendid liberality. *Farley* arranged the action; the painter and the mechanist, *Grieve* and (among the *mechanical* prophets!) *Saul,* contributed their art; and *Bishop* supplied the music, which (a circumstance equally *novel!*), was quite *new.*

These advantages, combined with the excellent acting of Liston, Farley, Mrs. Egerton, and Miss Booth, insured the Miller and his Men a brilliant reception. This melodrame is the production of Mr. Pocock, and was first produced at Covent Garden, on the 21st of October, 1813.

☞ D.——G.

Costume.

COUNT FREDERICK FRIBERG.—Green jacket —pantaloons, trimmed with silver—high green cap, trimmed with silver—russet boots—high gloves—sword and rocqulaine.

KARL.—Drab jacket and pantaloons, trimmed with dark binding—short cloak, over one shoulder, trimmed with dark binding—russet boots—high drab cap, with bagtail and cords to it—belt and sword.

GRINDOFF.—*First dress :* Light drab jerkin, with dark binding—white shirt, dark braces shown in front —white canvass trousers, with dark binding on the outside the leg—russet boots—light blue kerchief—large slouch beaver hat.—*Second dress :* Salmon-coloured pantaloons—dark tunic, with large brass plates and studs down the front—short russet ankle-boots, with small tops turned over—a long dark cloak—dark brown cap, and small feather.

KELMAR.—Drab jerkin—breeches, bound with brown—leather belt and brass buckles—brown cloak, trimmed with fur—blue worsted stockings—russet shoes, and brown cap, bound with fur.

LOTHAIR.—*First dress :* Black worsted pantaloons —blue fly, with black buttons and binding—white shirt-sleeves—dark braces shown in front—russet sandals—

black cap.—*Second dress :* Dark brown jerkin—slashed trunks—dark cloak—the whole dress patched and torn —flesh leggings—russet boots—long black wig—belt and buckle—face discoloured.

RIBER.—Brown leather jerkins—dark slashed trunks —gauntlets—flesh leggings—black cap—red feathers— goat skin and dark brown cloak—belt and' buckle— russet and goat-skin short boots.

GOLOTZ.—Ibid.

KRUITZ.—Brown jerkin—trunks—flesh leggings.

ROBBERS.—*First dress :* Millers' frocks—trousers —white hats.—*Second dress :* Various darkly-coloured jerkins—trunks—cloaks—flesh leggings—boots—caps— belts—swords—pistols—daggers—bugle-horns, &c.

CLAUDINE.—Buff petticoat, trimmed with red and black—an apron trimmed with coloured ribbon—blue body, trimmed—white sleeves, ringed with coloured ribbon up the arm.

RAVINA.—Drab petticoat—short dark red tunic— flesh-coloured stockings—sandals.

LAURETTE.—Coloured body and petticoat—apron.

Cast of the Characters,

As Performed at the Theatre Royal, Covent Garden.

	Original.	1830.
Grindoff, the Miller	Mr. Farley.	Mr. Farley.
Count Frederick Friberg . . .	Mr. Vining.	Mr. Horrebow.
Karl, his Servant	Mr. Liston.	Mr. Blanchard.
Lothair, a young Peasant . . .	Mr. Abbott.	Mr. Duruset.
Kelmar, an old Cottager . . .	Mr. Chapman.	Mr. Evans
Kruitz, his Son	Mast. Gladstanes.	Master Watson.
Riber, }	M. Jefferies.	Mr. Henry.
Golotz, } Banditti . .	Mr. King.	Mr. Mears.
Zingra, }	Mr. Slader.	Mr. Norris
Claudine, } Kelmar's Daughters	Miss Booth.	Mrs. Vining.
Laurette, }	Miss Carew.	Mrs. Brown.
Ravina	Mrs. Egerton.	Miss Lacy.

The Miller's Men, Banditti, Officers of Count Friberg, &c. &c.

SCENE,—The Banks of a River on the Borders of a Forest in Bohemia.

THE MILLER AND HIS MEN.

ACT I.

SCENE I.—*The Banks of a River   On the right, in the distance, a rocky eminence, on which is a windmill at work—a cottage in front,* R. S. E.—*Sunset.*

MUSIC.—THE MILLER'S MEN *are seen in perspective, descending the eminence—they cross the river in boats, and land near the cottage, with their sacks, singing the following*

ROUND.

When the wind blows,
    When the mill goes,
Our hearts are all light and merry ;
    When the wind drops,
    When the mill stops,
We drink and sing, hey down derry.
    [*Exeunt, two in the boat,* R. U. E., *the rest,* R.

Enter KELMAR, *from the cottage,* R. S. E.

Kel. What ! more sacks, more grist to the mill ! early and late the miller thrives ; he that was my tenant is now my landlord ; this hovel, that once sheltered him, is now the only dwelling of bankrupt broken-hearted Kelmar—well, I strove my best against misfortune, and, thanks be to heaven, have fallen respected, even by my enemies.

Enter CLAUDINE, *with a basket,* L. S. E.

So, Claudine, you are returned.   Where stayed you so long ?

Cla. I was obliged to wait ere I could cross the ferry —there were other passenges.

Kel. (R. C.) Amongst whom I suppose was one in whose company time flew so fast—the sun had set before you had observed it.

Cla. (L. C.) No, indeed, father : since you desired me to meet Lothair—and I told him what you had desired—I have never seen him but in the cottage here, when you were present.

Kel. You are a good girl—a dutiful child, and I believe you—you never yet deceived me.

Cla. Nor ever will, dear father—but——

Kel. But what?

Cla. I—I find it very lonely passing the borders of the forest without— without——

Kel. Without Lothair?

Cla. You know, 'tis dangerous, father.

Kel. Not half so dangerous as love—subdue it, child, in time.

Cla. But the robbers !

Kel. Robbers ! what then ?—they cannot injure thee or thy father—alas ! we have no more to lose—yet thou hast one treasure left, innocence !—guard well thy heart, for should the fatal passion there take root, 'twill rob thee of thy peace.

Cla. You told me, once, love's impulse could not be resisted.

Kel. When the object is worthless, it should not be indulged.

Cla. Is Lothair worthless?

Kel. No ; but he is poor almost as you are.

Cla. Do riches without love give happiness?

Kel. Never.

Cla. Then I must be unhappy if I wed the miller Grindoff.

Kel. Not so—not so ;—independence gives comfort, but love without competence is endless misery. You can never wed Lothair.

Cla. [*Sighing.*] I can never love the miller.

Kel. Then you shall never marry him—though to see you Grindoff's wife be the last wish of your old father's heart. Go in, child ; go in, Claudine. [*Claudine kisses his hand, and exit into the cottage,* R. S. E.] 'Tis plain her heart is rivetted to Lothair, and honest Grindoff yet must sue in vain.

Enter LOTHAIR, *hastily*, L. S. E.

Lot. Ah! Kelmar, and alone!—where is Claudine?

Kel. At home, in her father's house,—where should she be?

Lot. Then she has escaped—she is safe, and I happy—I did not accompany her in vain.

Kel. Accompany!—accompany!—Has she then told me a falsehood? Were you with her, Lothair?

Lot. No—ye—yes. [*Aside.*] I must not alarm him.

Kel. (R.) What mean these contradictions?

Lot. She knew not I was near her—you have denied our meeting, but you cannot prevent my loving her—I have watched her daily through the village and along the borders of the forest.

Kel. I thank you; but she needs no guard; her poverty will protect her from a thief.

Lot. (L.) Will her beauty protect her from a libertine?

Kel. Her virtue will.

Lot. I doubt it:—what can her resistance avail against the powerful arm of villany?

Kel. Is there such a wretch?

Lot. There is.

Kel. Lothair, Lothair! I fear you glance at the miller Grindoff. This is not well; this is not just.

Lot. Kelmar, you wrong me; 'tis true, he is my enemy, for he bars my road to happiness. Yet I respect his character; the riches that industry has gained him he employs in assisting the unfortunate—he has protected you and your child, and I honour him.

Kel. If not to Grindoff, to whom did you allude?

Lot. Listen:—as I crossed the hollow way in the forest, I heard a rustling in the copse. Claudine had reached the bank above. As I was following, voices, subdued and whispering, struck my ear. Her name was distinctly pronounced: "She comes," said one; "Now! now we may secure her," cried the second; and instantly two men advanced; a sudden exclamation burst from my lips, and arrested their intent; they turned to seek me, and with dreadful imprecations vowed death to the intruder. Stretched beneath a bush of holly, I lay concealed; they passed within my reach; I scarcely breathed, while I observed them to be ruffians, uncouth and savage—they were banditti.

B 3

Kel. Banditti! are they not yet content? All that I had—all that the hand of Providence had spared, they have deprived me of; and would they take my child?

Lot. 'Tis plain they. would. Now, Kelmar, hear the last proposal of him you have rejected. I'll seek these robbers! if I should fall, your daughter will more readily obey your wish, and become the wife of Grindoff. If I should succeed, promise her to me. The reward I shall receive will secure our future comfort, and thus your fears and your objections both are satisfied.

Kel. [*Affected.*] Lothair, thou art a good lad, a noble lad, and worthy my daughter's love; she had been freely thine, but that by sad experience I know how keen the pangs of penury are to a parent's heart.

Lot. Then you consent?

Kel. I do, I do; but pray be careful. I fear 'tis a rash attempt: you must have help.

Lot. Then, indeed, I fail as others have before me. No, Kelmar, I must go alone, pennyless, unarmed, and secretly. None but yourself must know my purpose, or my person.

Kel. Be it as you will; but pray be careful; come, thou shalt see her.   [*The mill stops.*

Lot. I'll follow; it may be my last farewell.

Kel. Come in—I see the mill has stopped. Grindoff will be here anon; he always visits me at night-fall, when labour ceases. Come.

[*Exit Kelmar into the cottage*, R. S. E.

Lot. Yes, at the peril of my life, I'll seek them. With the juice of herbs my face shall be discoloured, and, in the garb of misery, I'll throw myself within their power —the rest I leave to Providence. [Music.] But the miller comes.

[*Exit to the cottage*, R. S. E.—*the Miller appears in perspective coming from the crag in the rock—the boat disappears on the opposite side.*

Enter the two Robbers, RIBER *and* GOLOTZ, *hastily*, R. S. E. —*they rush up to the cottage*, L. S. E., *and peep in at the window.*

Rib. [*Retiring from the window.*] We are too late— she has reached the cottage.

Gol. Curse on the interruption that detained us; we shall be rated for this failure.

Rib. (R.) Hush! not so loud. [*Goes again cautiously to the window of the cottage.*] Ha! Lothair.

Gol. (L.) Lothair! 'twas he, then, that marred our purpose; he shall smart for't.

Rib. Back! back! he comes.   On his return he dies; he cannot pass us both.

Music.—They retire behind a tree, L. U. E.—*A boat passes in the distance from the mouth of the cavern in the rock beneath the mill,* L. U. E., *to* R. U. E., *and then draws up to the bank—Enter* GRINDOFF, THE MILLER, *in the boat, who jumps ashore,* I.

Re-enter LOTHAIR, *at the same moment, from the cottage,* R. S. E.

Gri. (L.) [*Disconcerted.*] Lothair!

Lot. (R.) Ay, my visit here displeases you, no doubt.

Gri. Nay, we are rivals, but not enemies, I trust. We love the same girl; we strive the best we can to gain her: if you are fortunate, I'll wish you joy with all my heart; if I should have the luck on't, you'll do the same by me, I hope.

Lot. You have little fear; I am poor, you are rich. He needn't look far that would see the end on't.

Gri. But you are young and likely. I am honest and rough; the chances are as much your's as mine.

Lot. Well, time will show. I bear you no enmity. Farewell!   [*Crosses to* L.

Gri. (R.) [*Aside.*] He must not pass the forest. [*To Lothair.*] Whither go you?

Lot. (L.) To the village; I must haste, or 'twill be late ere I reach the ferry.   [*It begins to grow dark.*

Rib. [*Who with Golotz is watching them from* L. U. E.] He will escape us yet.

Gri. (L. C.) Stay, my boat shall put you across the river. Besides, the evening looks stormy—come, it will save your journey half a league.

Rib. [*Aside,* L. U. E.] It will save his life.

Lot. Well, I accept your offer, and I thank you.

Gri. Your hand.

Lot. Farewell!

           [*He goes into the boat, and pushes off,* R. U. E.

Gri. So, I am rid of him; if he had met Claudine!—but she is safe—now, then, for Kelmar.

[*Exit into the cottage,* R. S. E.

Re-enter RIBER *and* GOLOTZ, L. U. E.

Rib. Curse on this chance! we have lost him!
Gol. But a time may come.
Rib. A time shall come, and shortly, too.

[*Exeunt,* L. S. E.

SCENE II.—*The Forest—distant thunder—stage dark.*

Enter KARL, *dragging after him a portmanteau,* L.

Karl. Here's a pretty mess! here's a precious spot of work!—Pleasant, upon my soul—lost in a labyrinth, without love or liquor—the sun gone down, a storm got up, and no getting out of this vile forest, turn which way one will.

Count. [*Calling without,* L.] Halloo! Karl! Karl!

Karl. Ah, you may call and bawl, master of mine; you'll not disturb any thing here but a wild boar or two, and a wolf, perhaps.

Enter COUNT FREDERICK FRIBERG, L.

Count. Karl, where are you?
Karl. (R.) Where am I! that's what I want to know—this cursed wood has a thousand turnings, and not one that turns right.

Count. (L.) Careless coxcomb! said you not you could remember the track?

Karl. So I should, sir, if I could find the path—but trees will grow, and since I was here last, the place has got so busby and briery, that—that I have lost my way.

Count. You have lost your senses.

Karl. No, sir, I wish I had; unfortunately, my senses are all in the highest state of perfection.

Count. Why not use them to more effect?

Karl. I wish I'd the opportunity; my poor stomach can testify that I taste——

Count. What?

Karl. Nothing; it's as empty as my head: but I see danger, smell a tempest, hear the cry of wild beasts, and feel——

Count. How?

Karl. Particularly unpleasant. [*Thunder and rain.*] Oh, we are in for it: do you hear, sir?

Count. We must be near the river; could we but reach the ferry, 'tis but a short league to the Chateau Friberg.   [*Crosses,* R.

Karl. (R.) Ah, sir, I wish we were there, and I seated in the old arm-chair in the servant's hall talking of—holloa!

Count. (L.) What now?

Karl, I felt a spot of rain on my nose as big as a bullet. [*Thunder and rain.*] There, there, it's coming on again—seek some shelter, sir; some hollow tree, whilst I, for my sins, endeavour once more to find the way, and endure another curry-combing among these cursed brambles.   Come, sir. [*The storm increases.*] Lord, how it rumbles—this way, sir—this way.   [*Exeunt,* R.

SCENE III.—*A Room in the Cottage. A Door,* R. F. *A Window,* L. F. *A Fire,* R. S. E.—*tables,* R. *and* L.—*chairs, &c.*

GRINDOFF, L., *and* KELMAR, R., *discovered sitting at the table,* R.—*Thunder and rain.*

Kel. 'Tis a rough night, miller: the thunder roars, and, by the murmuring of the flood, the mountain torrents have descended. Poor Lothair! he'll scarcely have crossed the ferry.

Gri. Lothair by this is safe at home, old friend; before the storm commenced, I passed him in my boat across the river. [*Aside.*] He seems less anxious for his daughter than for this bold stripling.

Kel. Worthy man! you'll be rewarded for all such deeds hereafter. Thank heaven, Claudine is safe! Hark!   [*Thunder heard.*

Gri. [*Aside.*] She is safe by this time, or I am much mistaken.

Kel. She will be here anon.

Gri. [*Aside.*] I doubt that. [*To Kelmar.*] Come, here's health, old Kelmar,—here's Claudine!   [*Drinks.*

Kel. Claudine,—heaven bless her !   [*Drinks.*

Gri. Ah, Kelmar, would I could once call you father !

Kel. You may do soon ; but even your protection would now, I fear, be insufficient to——

Gri. What mean you ?—Insufficient !

Kel. The robbers—this evening in the forest——

Gri. [*Rising.*] Ha ?

Kel. [*Rising.*] Did not Lothair, then, tell you ?

Gri. Lothair ?

Kel. Yes ; but all's well ; be not alarmed—see, she is here.

Gri. Here !

Enter CLAUDINE, R.—*Grindoff endeavours to suppress his surprise.*

Gri. Claudine !   Curse on them both !

Kel. (c.) Both ! how knew you there were two ?

Gri. (L.) 'Sdeath !—you—you said robbers, did you not ? They never have appeared but singly ; therefore, I thought you meant two.

Kel. You are right ; but for Lothair they had deprived me of my child.

Gri. How !—Did Lothair ? Humph ! he's a courageous youth.

Cla. That he is ; but he's gentle, too.   What has happened ?

Kel. Nothing, child, nothing. [*Aside to Grindoff.*] Do not speak on't, 'twill terrify her.   Come, Claudine, now for supper.   What have you brought us ?

Cla. Thanks to the miller's bounty, plenty.

Kel. The storm increases !

Karl. [*Calling without,* R. D. F.] Holloa ! Holloa !

Kel. And hark ! There a voice—listen !

Karl. [*Calling again without,* R. D. F.] Holloa !

Cla. The cry of some bewildered traveller.

[*The cry repeated, and a violent knock at the door,* R. F.

Kel. Open the door.

Gri. Not so ; it may be dangerous.

Kel. Danger comes in silence and in secret ; my door was never shut against the wretched while I knew prosperity, nor shall it be closed now to my fellows in misfortune. [*To Claudine.*] Open the door, I say.

[*The knock is repeated, and Claudine opens the door.*

Enter KARL, R. D. F., *with a portmanteau.*

Karl. (C.) Why, in the name of dark nights and tempests, didn't you open the door at first!—Have you no charity?

Kel. (R. C.) In our hearts plenty, in our gift but little; yet all we have is yours.

Karl. Then I'll share all you have with my master: thank you, old gentleman; you wont fare the worse for sheltering honest Karl, and Count Frederick Friberg.

Gri. (L.) Friberg!

Karl. Ay, I'll soon fetch him; he's waiting now, looking as melancholy as a mourning-coach in a snow-storm, at the foot of a tree, wet as a drowned rat; so stir up the fire, bless you! clap on the kettle, give us the best eatables and drinkables you have, a clean table-cloth, a couple of warm beds, and don't stand upon ceremony; we'll accept every civility and comfort you can bestow upon us without scruple.

[*Throws down the portmanteau,* C., *and exit,* R. D. F.

Gri. (L.) Friberg, did he say?

Cla. (R.) 'Tis the young count, so long expected.

Kel. (R. C.) Can it be possible? without attendants, and at such a time, too?

Gri. [*Looking at the portmanteau, on which is the name in brass nails.*] It must be the same!—Kelmar, good night.   [*Going up towards the door.*

Kel. Nay, not yet,—the storm rages.

Gri. I fear, it may increase; besides, your visitors may not like my company; good night.

Enter COUNT FREDERICK FRIBERG, R. D. F., *followed by* KARL—*he stops suddenly, and eyes the Miller, as if recollecting him—Grindoff appears to avoid his scrutiny.*

Count. Your kindness is well timed; we might have perished; accept my thanks. [*Aside.*] I should know that face.

Gri. (L.) To me your thanks are not due.

Count. That voice, too!

Gri. This house is Kelmar's.

[*Karl places the portmanteau on the table,* L. U. E.

Count. Kelmar's!

Kel. Ay, my dear master: my fortunes have deserted me, but my attachment to your family still remains.

Count. Worthy old man, how happens this : the richest tenant of my late father's land, the honest, the faithful Kelmar, in a hovel ?

Kel. It will chill your hearts to hear.

Karl. [*At the fire, drying and warming himself.*] Then don't tell us, pray, for our bodies are cramped with cold already.

Kel. 'Tis a terrible tale.

Karl. [*Advancing,* L. C.] Then, for the love of a good appetite and a dry skin, don't tell it, for I've been terrified enough in the forest to-night to last me my life.

Count. Be silent, Karl. [*Retires up,* R., *with Kelmar.*

Gri. (L.) In—in the forest?

Karl. (R.) Ay.

Gri. What should alarm you there ?

Karl. What should alarm me there ? come, that's a good one. Why, first, I lost my way ; trying to find that, I lost the horses ; then I tumbled into a quagmire, and nearly lost my life.

Gri. Psha! this is of no consequence.

Kar. Isn't it ? I have endured more hardships since morning than a knight-errant. My head's broken, my body's bruised, and my joints are dislocated. I hav'nt three square inches about me but what are scarified with briers and brambles ; and, above all, I have not tasted a morsel of food since sunrise. Egad ! instead of my making a meal of anything, I've been in constant expectation of the wolves making a meal of me.

Gri. Is this all ?

Karl. All!—No, it's not all ; pretty well, too, I think. When I recovered the path, I met two polite gentlemen with long knives in their hands.

Gri. Hey !

Karl. And because I refused a kind invitation of theirs, they were affronted, and were just on the point of ending all my troubles, when up came my master.

Gri. Well ?

Karl. Well ! yes, it was well indeed, for after a struggle they made off ; one of them left his sting behind, though ; look, here's a poker to stir up a man's courage with !   [*Showing a poniard.*

Gri. A poniard !

Karl. Ay.

Gri. [*Snatching at it.*] Give it me.

Karl. [*Refusing the dagger.*] For what? It's lawful spoil—didn't I win it in battle? No! I'll keep it as a trophy of my victory.

> [*During this time, Kelmar and Claudine have taken and hung up the Count's cloak, handed him a chair, and are conversing.*

Gri. It will be safer in my possession: it may lead to a discovery of him who wore it—and——

Karl. It may—you are right—therefore I'll deliver it into the hands of Count Frederick: he'll soon ferret the rascals out; set a reward on their heads—five thousand crowns, dead or alive! that's the way to manœuvre 'em.

Gri. Indeed! humph!   [*Turns up,* L.

Karl. Humph! don't half like that chap—never saw such a ferocious black muzzle in my life—that miller's a rogue in grain.

Count. [*Advancing,* c.] Nay, nay, speak of it no more. I will not take an old man's bed to ease my youthful limbs; I have slept soundly on a ruder couch—and that chair shall be my resting-place.

Cla. The miller's man, Riber, perhaps can entertain his excellency better;—he keeps the Flask here, on the hill, sir.

Gri. (L. C.) His house contains but one bed.

Karl. (L.) Only one?

Gri. And that is occupied.

Karl. The devil it is!

Count. It matters not; I am contented here.

Karl. That's more than I am.   [*Retires up,* L.

Gri. But stay: perchance his guest has left it; if so, 'tis at Count Frederick's service. [*They all retire up but Grindoff.*] I'll go directly and bring you word. [*Aside.*] I may now prevent surprise—the storm has ceased; I will return immediately.

> [*Throws down the sheath of a dagger,* c., *and exit,* R. D. F.

Count. [*Eagerly.*] Kelmar, tell me, who is that man?

Kel. [*Advancing.*] The richest tenant, sir, you have; what Kelmar was when you departed from Bohemia, Grindoff now is.

Count. Grindoff!—I remember, in my youth, a favoured servant of my father's, who resembled him in countenance and voice—the recollection is strong upon my

c

memory, but I hope deceives me, for he was a villain who betrayed his trust.

Kel. (L. C.) I have heard the cirumstance; it happened just before I entered your good father's service—his name was Wolf.

Count. The same.

Karl. (L.) And if this is not the same, I suspect he is a very near relation.

Kel. [*Angrily.*] Nay, sir, you mistake—Grindoff is my friend,—come, Claudine, is all ready?

Karl. Oh, it's a sore subject, is it? [*Exeunt Kelmar and Claudine,* R.] Your friend, is he, old gentleman?— Sir—sir——

Count. [*Who has become thoughtful.*] Well! what say you?

Karl. I don't like our quarters, sir; we are in a bad neighbourhood.

Count. (R.) I fear we are; Kelmar's extreme poverty may have tempted him to league with—yet his daughter.

Karl. (L.) His daughter—a decoy!—nothing but a trap; don't believe her, sir; we are betrayed, murdered, if we stay here. I'll endure anything, every thing, if you will but depart, sir. Dark nights, bad roads, hail, rain, assassins, and—hey! what's this? [*Sees and picks up the scabbard dropped by Grindoff.*] Oh, lord, what's the matter with me? My mind misgives me; and here [*He sheathes the dagger in it and finds it fit.*] fits to a hair—we are in the lion's den!

Count. 'Tis evident, we are snared, caught.

Karl. O, lord! don't say so.

Re-enter KELMAR *and* CLAUDINE, *followed by* LAURETTE *and* KRUITZ *with supper things, &c.* R.

Kel. Come, come, youngsters, bestir—spread the cloth, and——

Count. Kelmar, I have bethought me; at every peril, I must on to-night.

Kel. To-night!

Cla. Not to-night, I beseech you; you know not half your danger.

[*Goes to the table,* L., *and places her hand carelessly on the portmanteau*

Karl. Danger! [*Aside.*] Cockatrice! [*To Claudine.*] I'll thank you for that portmanteau.

Count. Let it remain—it may be an object to them, 'tis none to me,—it will be safer here with honest Kelmar.

Kel. But why so sudden?

Karl. My master has recollected something that must be done to-night—or to-morrow it may be out of his power.

Cla. (R.) Stay till the miller returns.

Karl. Till he returns! [*Aside.*] Ah, the fellow's gone to get assistance, and if he comes before we escape, we shall be cut and hashed to mince-meat.

Count. Away!　　　　　　　　[*Advancing to the door.*

Enter GRINDOFF, *suddenly*, R. D. F.

Karl. It's all over with us.

Kel. Well, friend, what success?

Gri. Bad enough—the count must remain here.

Count. Must remain!

Gri. There is no resource.

Karl. I thought so.

Gri. To-morrow, Riber can dispose of you both.

Karl. Dispose of us! [*Aside.*] Ay, put us to bed with a spade—that fellow's a grave-digger.

Count. Then I must cross the ford to-night.

Gri. Impossible; the torrent has swept the ferry barge from the shore.

Kel. The ferry barge!

Gri. Yes, and driven it down the stream.

Count. Perhaps, your boat—

Gri. Mine! 'twould be madness to resist the current now—and in the dark, too.

Count. What reward may tempt you?

Gri. Not all you are worth, sir, until to-morrow.

Karl. To-morrow!—[*Aside.*] Ah! we are crow's meat, to a certainty.

Gri. [*Aside, looking askance around the room.*] All is right: they have got the scabbard, and their suspicions now must fall on Kelmar.

　　[*Exit Grindoff*, R. D. F. *bidding them all good night.*

Count. Well, we must submit to circumstances. [*Aside to Karl.*] Do not appear alarmed; when all is still, we may escape.

Karl. Why not now ? There are only two of 'em.
Count. There may be others near.

SESTETTE.

Cla.   Stay, prithee, stay—the night is dark,
      The cold wind whistles—hark ! hark ! hark !
Count. We must away.
Karl.   Pray, come away.
Cla.   The night is dark,
      The cold wind whistles.
All.   Hark ! hark ! hark !
Cla.   Stay, prithee, stay—the way is lone,
      The ford is deep—the boat is gone.
Kel.   And mountain torrents swell the flood,
      And robbers lurk within the wood.
All.   Here $\left\{ \begin{smallmatrix} \text{you} \\ \text{we} \end{smallmatrix} \right\}$ must stay till morning bright
      Breaks through the dark and dismal night,
      And merry sings the rising lark,
      And hush'd the night bird—hark ! hark ! hark !
   [*Claudine tenderly detains the Count—Kelmar detains
      Karl, and the scene closes.*

SCENE IV.—*The Depth of the Forest—Stage dark.*

Enter LOTHAIR, L., *with his dress and complexion entirely
   changed—his appearance is extremely wretched.*

Lot. This way, this—in the moaning of the blast,
at intervals, I heard the tread of feet—and as the
moon's light burst from the stormy clouds, I saw two
figures glide like departed spirits to this deep glen.
Now, heaven prosper me, for my attempt is desperate !
[*Looking off*, R.] ah, they come !   [*Retires*, R. S. E.

Music.—*Enter* RIBER, R., GOLOTZ *follows—they look
   around cautiously, then advance to a particular rock,* L. F.,
   *which is nearly concealed by underwood and roots of
   trees.*

Lot. [*Advancing*, R.] Hold ! [*The Robbers start, and
eye him with ferocious surprise.*] So, my purpose is accomplished—at last I have discovered you.

Rib. [*Crosses, c.*] Indeed! it will cost you dear.

Lot. It has already—I have been hunted through the country—but now my life is safe.

Rib. Safe!

Lot. Ay, is it not? Would you destroy a comrade ?—Look at me, search me—I am unarmed, defenceless!

Gol. Why come you hither?

Lot. To join your brave band—the terror of Bohemia.

Rib. How knew you our retreat?

Lot. No matter—in the service of Count Friberg I have been disgraced—and fly from punishment to seek revenge.

Gol. [*To Riber.*] How say you ?

Lot. [*Aside.*] They hesitate, the young count is far from home, and his name I may use without danger. [*To the Robbers.*] Lead me to your chief.

Rib. We will—not so fast, your sight must be concealed.   [*Offering to bind his forehead.*

Lot. Ah! [*Hesitates.*] May I trust you ?

Gol. Do you doubt ?

Rib. Might we not despatch you as you are.

Lot. Enough ; bind me, and lead on.

                            [*They conceal his sight.*
[*Music.—Golotz leads Lothair to the rock,* L., *pushes the brushwood aside, and all exeunt, followed by Riber, watching that they are not observed.*

SCENE VI.—*A Cavern.*

BANDITTI *discovered variously employed, chiefly sitting carousing around tables on which are flasks of wine, &c. —steps rudely cut in the rock, in the background, leading to an elevated recess, c. on which is inscribed "* POW-DER MAGAZINE.*"—Other steps lead to an opening in the cave—a grated door,* R.—*stage light.*

CHORUS.—BANDITTI.

Fill, boys, and drink about,—
  Wine will banish sorrow ;
Come, drain the goblet out,—
  We'll have more to-morrow.
            [*The Robbers all rise and come forward.*
                    3

Slow Movement.

We live free from fear,
In harmony here,
Combin'd, just like brother and brother ;
And this be our toast,
The free-booter's boast,
Success, and good·will to each other !
Chorus.   Fill, boys, &c.

Enter RAVINA, *through the grated door,* R., *as they con-*
clude.

Rav. What, carousing yet, sotting yet !

Zin. How now, Ravina ; why so churlish ?

Rav. To sleep, I say—or wait upon yourselves. I'll stay no longer from my couch to please you. Is it not enough that I toil from day-break, but you must disturb me ever with your midnight revelry ?

Zin. You were not wont to be so savage, woman.

Rav. (R. C.) You were not wont to be so insolent. Look you repent it not.

First Robber. (L. C.) Psha ! heed her no more. Jea-loury hath soured her.

Zin. I forgive her railing.

Rav. Forgive !

Zin. Ay ; our leader seeks another mistress, and 'tis rather hard upon thee, I confess, after five years' capti-vity, hard service, too, and now that you are accus-tomed to our way of life—we pity thee.

Rav. Pity me ! I am indeed an object of compassion ; seven long years a captive, hopeless still of liberty. Miserable lost Ravina! by dire necessity become an agent in their wickedness, yet I pine for virtue and for freedom.

Zin. Leave us to our wine.

[*A single note on the bugle is heard from below,* R. U. E.

Zin. Hark ! 'tis from the lower cave. [*Note repeated*] She comes ; Ravina, look you receive her as becomes the companion of our chief—remember.

Rav. I shall remember. [*Crosses,* L.] So, another vic-tim to hypocrisy and guilt. Poor wretch ! she loves,

perhaps, as I did, the miller Grindoff; but, as I do, may
live to execrate the outlaw and the robber.

       [Music.—The trap in the floor is thrown open.

Enter RIBER, *through the floor, followed by* GOLOTZ *and*
      LOTHAIR—*they all advance,* R.

  Robbers. Hail to our new companion !
  Rav. (L.) A man !
*[Lothair tears the bandage from his eyes as he arrives in
  the cave—the Robbers start back on perceiving a man.*
  Lot. Thanks for your welcome.
  Zin. Who have we here?—Speak !
  Rib. A recruit; where is the captain ?
 ·*Zin.* Where is the captain's bride ?
  Rib. Of her hereafter. [*A bugle is heard above,* L. U. E.
  Robbers. Wolf! Wolf!

Enter GRINDOFF, *in robber's apparel—he descends the
    opening, and advances*

Zin.
  &* *}* Welcome, noble captain !
Robbers.
 —*Gri.* [*Starts at seeing Lothair*] A stranger !
  Lot. [*Aside.*] Grindoff !
         [*The Robbers lay hands on their swords, &c.*
 —*Gri.* Ha! betray'd! who has done this ?
  Rib. [*Advancing,* C.] I brought him hither, to——
  Gri. Riber! humph! You have executed my orders
well, have you not?—Where is Claudine ?
  Lot. (R.) Claudine! [*Aside.*] Villain! hypocrite!
 —*Gri.* Know you Claudine, likewise ?
  Rib. She escaped us in the forest—some meddling
fool thwarted our intent, and——
  Gri. Silence, I know it all; a word with you pre-
sently : now, stranger—[*Crossing to Lothair.*] but I mis-
take; we should be old acquaintance—my name is so
familiar to you : what is your purpose here ?
  Lot. Revenge.
 —*Gri.* On whom?
  Lot. On one whose cruelty and oppression well de-
serve it.
 —*Gri.* His name?
  Lot. [*Aside.*] Would I dare mention it!
 —*Gri.* His name, I say ?

Rib.- He complains of Count Friberg.

Gri. Indeed! then your purpose will be soon accomplished: he arrived this night, and shelters at old Kelmar's cottage; he shall never pass the river; should he once reach the Chateau Friberg, it would be fatal to our band.

Lot. Arrived! [*Aside.*] What have I done! My fatal indiscretion has destroyed him. [*To Grindoff.*] Let him fall by my hand.

Gri. It may tremble—it trembles now. The firmest of our band have failed. [*Looking at Riber.*] Henceforth the enterprise shall be my own.

               [*Ravina goes behind to* R.

Lot. Let me accompany you.

Gri. Not to-night.

Lot. To-night!

Gri. Ay, before the dawn appears, he dies—Riber!

     [*Lothair clasps his hands in agony—Riber advances.*

Rav. What, more blood! must Friberg's life be added to the list?

Gri. It must; our safety claims it.

Rav. Short-sighted man! will not his death doubly arouse the sluggish arm of justice?—The whole country, hitherto kept in awe by dissension and selfish fear, will join; reflect in time; beware their retribution!

Gri. When I need a woman's help and counsel, I'll seek it of the compassionate Ravina. Begone! [*Turning to Riber.*] Riber, I say!   [*Exit Ravina,* R. D.

Rib. I wait your orders.

Gri. Look you execute them better than the last—look to't—the Count and his companion rest at Kelmar's; it must be done within an hour: arm, and attend me: at the same time, I will secure Claudine; and, should Kelmar's vigilance interpose to mar us, he henceforth shall be an inmate here.

Lot. (R.) Oh, villain!

Gri. [*Rushing towards Lothair.*] How mean you?

Lot. Friberg—let me go with you.

Gri. You are too eager; I will not trust thy inexperience: trust you! what surety have we of your faith?

Lot. My oath.

Gri. Swear, then, never to desert the object, never to betray the cause for which you sought our band—revenge on——

Lot. On him who has deeply, basely injured me, I swear it.

Gri. 'Tis well—your name?

Lot. Spiller!

Gri. [*To Riber.*] Quick, arm, and attend me. [*Riber retires,* R.] Are those sacks in the mill disposed of as I ordered!

Zin. They are, captain.

Gri. Return with the flour to-morrow, and be careful that all assume the calmness of industry and content. With such appearance, suspicion itself is blind; 'tis the safeguard of our band. Fill me a horn, and then to business. [*A Robber hands him a horn of wine—he drinks.*] The Miller and his Men!

Robbers. [*Drinking.*] The Miller and his Men!

[*Grindoff and Robbers laugh heartily—Grindoff puts on his miller's frock, hat, &c.—Riber, armed with pistols in his belt, advances with a dark lantern, and exeunt with Grindoff through the rock,* L. F.

CHORUS—BANDITTI.

Now to the forest we repair,
Awhile like spirits wander there;
In darkness we secure our prey,
And vanish at the dawn of day.

END OF ACT I.

J.W.Roberts.

ACT II.

SCENE I.—*The Interior of Kelmar's Cottage, as before.* COUNT FREDERICK FRIBERG *discovered asleep in a chair, reclining on a table near* L. S. E*, and at the opposite side, near the fire, Karl is likewise seen asleep,* R.—*the Count's sword lies on the table,* L.—*the fire is nearly extinguished—stage dark—Music as the curtain rises.*

Enter CLAUDINE, *with a lamp, down the stairs,* L. S. E.

Cla. All still, all silent! the Count and his companions are undisturbed!—What can it mean?—My father wanders from his bed, restless as myself. Alas! the infirmities of age and sorrow afflict him sorely. Night after night I throw myself upon a sleepless couch, ready to fly to his assistance, and—hush—hush!

Enter KELMAR, R.—*Claudine extinguishes the light, and avoids him,* L. S. E.

Kel. They sleep—sleep soundly—ere they awake, I may return from my inquiry. If Grindoff's story was correct, I still may trust him— still may the Count confide in him—but his behaviour last night, unusual and mysterious, hangs like a fearful dream upon my mind— his anxiety to leave the cottage, his agitation at the appearance of Count Friberg—but, above all, his assertion that the ferry-barge was lost, disturbs me. My doubts shall soon be ended. At this lone hour I may pass the borders unperceived, and the gray dawn that now glimmers in the east will direct my path.
[*Looks about him, fearful of disturbing the sleepers, and exit,* R. D. F.

Cla. [*Advancing,* c.] My father appears unusually agitated. Ah, it may be! sometimes he wanders on the river's brink, watching the bright orb of day bursting from the dark trees, and breathes a prayer, a blessing for his child; yet 'tis early, very early—yet it may be— Oh, father, my dear, dear father! [*Exit,* R. D. F.

Karl. Yaw! [*Snoring.*] Damn the rats! Yaw, what a noise they keep up! Hey, where am I?—Oh, in this infernal hovel; the night-mare has rode me into a jelly; then such horrible dreams, yaw! [*A light from the dark lantern borne by Riber is seen passing the window,* L. F.] and such a swarm of rats—damn the rats! [*Lays his hand on his poniard.*] They'd better keep off, for I'm hungry enough to eat one. Bew—eu! [*Shivering.*] I wish it were morning. [*Music.*

Enter RIBER, R. D. F.,—*he suddenly retires, observing a light occasioned by Karl's stirring the fire with his dagger.*

Karl. What's that? [*Listens.*] Nothing but odd noises all night: wonder how my master can sleep for such a—yaw—aw! Damn the rats! [*Lies down.*

MUSIC.—*Enter* RIBER *cautiously,* R. D. F., *holding forward the lantern*—GRINDOFF *follows. Riber, on seeing the Count, draws a poniard—he raises his arm, Grindoff catches it, and prevents the blow. Appropriate music.*

Gri. Not yet; first secure my prize, Claudine; these are safe.

Karl. How the varmint swarm!

Gri. Hush! he dreams.

Rib. It shall be his last.

Karl. Rats, rats!

Rib. What says he?

Karl. Rats!—they all come from the mill.

Rib. Do they so?

Karl. Ay, set traps for 'em, poison 'em.

[*Riber, again attempting to advance, is detained by Grindoff*

Gri. Again so rash—remember!

Karl. I shall never forget that fellow in the forest.

Rib. Ha! do you mark?

Gri. Fear them not; be still till I return; he is sound; none sleep so hard as those that babble in their dreams. Stir not, I charge you; yet, should Kelmar—ay—should you hear a noise without, instantly despatch.

[*Exit Grindoff, up the stairs,* L. S. E.

Rib. Enough. [*Karl awakes again—he observes Riber, grasps his dagger, and, watching the motion of the robber, acts accordingly.*] This delay is madness, but I must obey. [*Looking at the priming of his pistol, then towards the table—Karl drops his position.*] Hey, a sword! [*Advancing to the table,* L., *and removing the sword.*] Now, all is safe—Hark! [*A noise without, as of something falling.*] 'Tis time! if this should fail, my poniard will secure him.

[MUSIC.—*Riber advances hastily, and, in the act of bringing his pistol to the level against the Count, is stabbed by Karl, who has arisen and retreated behind the table to receive him.*

Enter GRINDOFF, L. S. E.—*the Count, rushing from the chair at the noise of the pistol, seizes him by the collar —the group stands amazed.*

Count. Speak! what means this?

Karl. [*Advancing.*] They've caught a tartar, sir, that's all.   Hey, the miller !

Gri. Ay !

Count. How came you here ?

Gri. (c.) To—to do you service.

Count. At such an hour !

Gri. 'Tis never too late to do good.

Count. Good !

Gri. Yes ; you have been in danger.

Karl. Have we ?   Thank you for your news.

Gri. You have been watched by the banditti.

Count. So it appears.

Karl. But how did you know it ?

Gri. [*Confused.*] There is my proof.

[*Pointing to the body of Riber.*

Karl. But how the plague got you into the house ?—Through a rat-hole ?

Count. Explain.

Gri. Few words will do that :—on my return to the mill, I found you might repose there better than in this house ; at all events, I knew you would be safer in my care.

Count. Safer !   Proceed ! what mean you ?

Karl. [*Aside.*] Safer !

Gri. Kelmar——

Count. Hah !

Gri. Had you no suspicion of him ?—no mistrust of his wish to—to detain you ?

Count. I confess, I——

Gri. [*To Karl.*] The poniard you obtained in the forest, that you refused to give me——

Karl. This ?

Gri. Is Kelmar's.

Count. Wretch !

Karl. I thought so ; I found the sheath here.

Gri. I knew it instantly ; my suspicions were aroused —now they are confirmed : Kelmar is in league with these marauders ; I found the door open,—you still slept.   I searched the house for him ; he is no where to be found,—he and his daughter have absconded.   Now, sir, are you satisfied ?

Count. I am.

Karl. I am not ; I wish we were safe at home,   I'm no coward by day-light, but I hate adventures of this kind in the dark.   Lord, how a man may be deceived !

I took you for a great rogue ; but I now find you are a
good Christian enough, though you are a very ill looking man.

Gri. Indeed ; we can't all be as handsome as you are,
you know.

Karl. [*Pertly.*] No ; nor as witty as you are, you
know.

Gri. Come, sir, follow me. [*Going up to door*, R. C.]
You can't mistake ; see, 'tis day-break : at the cottage
close to the narrow bridge that passes the ravine you
will find repose.

Count. We'll follow you. [*Exit Grindoff*, R. D. F.

Karl. I don't half like that fellow yet. [*Gets the portmanteau from* L. *table.*] Now, the sooner we are off the
better, sir. As for this fellow, the rats may take care
of him. [*Claudine's shrieks heard without*, R. D. F.

Fre. [*Drawing his sword.*] Ha ! a woman's voice !
Karl, follow me !

Karl. What, more adventures ! [*Drawing his sword.*]
I'm ready. I say, [*To the body of Riber.*] take care of
the portmanteau, will you ? [*Exit*, R. D. F.

SCENE II.—*The Forest—Stage partly dark.*

MUSIC.—*Enter* GRINDOFF, *with* CLAUDINE *in his arms.*

Count. [*Without*, R.] Karl ! Karl ! follow, this way !
Gri. [*Resting*, C.] Ha, so closely pursued !—Nay,
then——

[*Going hastily*, L., *he pushes aside the leaves of the
secret pass, and they disappear*, L.

Enter COUNT FREDERICK FRIBERG, *hastily*, R.

Count. Gone ! vanished ! Can it be possible ? Sure,
'tis witchcraft. I was close upon him—Karl ! The
cries of her he dragged with him, too, have ceas'd, and
not the faintest echo of his retiring footsteps can be
heard—Karl !

Enter Karl, R.

Karl. Oh, Lord ! Pho ! that hill's a breather ! Why,
where is he ? Didn't you overtake him :

Count. No! in this spot he disappeared, and sunk, as it should seem, ghost like, into the very earth.—Follow!

Kar. Follow!—Follow a will-o-the-wisp!

Count. Quick—aid me to search!

Karl. Search out a ghost!—Mercy on us! I'll follow you through the world, fight for you the best cock-giant robber of 'em all, but, if you're for hunting goblins, I'm off. Hey! where the devil's the woman, though? If she was a spirit, she made more noise than any lady alive.

Count. (L.) Perchance, the villain, so closely pursued, has destroyed his victim.

Karl. (R.) No doubt on't; he's killed her, to a certainty; nothing but death can stop a woman's tongue.

Count. [*Having searched in vain.*] From the miller we may gain assistance: Grindoff, no doubt, is acquainted with every turn and outlet of the forest;—quick, attend me to the mill.   [*Exeunt,* L.

SCENE III.—*The Cavern.*

MUSIC.—ROBBERS *discovered asleep in different parts, R. and* L.—LOTHAIR *on guard, with a carbine, stands beneath the magazine—stage partly light.*

Lot. (C.) Ere this it must be daylight—yet Grindoff returns not—perchance their foul intent has failed—the fatal blow designed for Friberg may have fallen upon himself. How tedious drags the time, when fear, suspense, and doubt thus weigh upon the heart. Oh, Kelmar, beloved Claudine, you little know my peril. [*Looks at the various groups of Banditti, and carefully rests his carbine at the foot of the rugged steps,* L. C., *leading to the magazine—he advances,* C.] While yet this drunken stupor makes their sleep most death-like, let me secure a terrible, but just revenge. If their infernal purpose be accomplished, this is their reward. [*Draws a coil of fusée from his bosom.*] These caverns, that spread beneath the mill, have various outlets, and in the fissures of the rock the train will lie unnoticed. Could I but reach the magazine!

[MUSIC.—*Lothair retires cautiously up,* C.—*he places his foot over the body of a Robber, who is seen asleep on the steps leading to the magazine—by accident he touches the carbine, which slips down—the Robber, being disturbed, alters his position, while Lothair stands over him, and again reposes — Lothair advances up the steps—as he arrives at the magazine, Wolf's signal, the bugle, is heard from above—the Robbers instantly start up, and Lothair, at the same moment, springs from the steps, and, seizing his carbine, stands in his previous attitude.*

Enter WOLF (GRINDOFF), *descending the steps of the opening,* L., *with* CLAUDINE *senseless in his arms.*

Robbers. The signal!

Gol. Wolf, we rejoice with you.

Lot. [*Advancing,* L.] Have you been successful?

Wolf. [*Setting down Claudine.*] So far, at least, I have.

Lot. [*Aside.*] Claudine—merciful powers! [*To Wolf.*] But Kelmar——

Wolf. Shall not long escape me—Kelmar once secure, his favourite, my redoubted rival, young Lothair, may next require attention—bear her in, Golotz. [*Golotz bears Claudine off.*] Where is Ravina?

Enter RAVINA, R. D.

Oh, you are come!

Rav. (R. C.) I am; what is your will?

Wolf. (L. C.) That you attend Claudine; treat her as you would treat me.

Rav. I will, be sure on't,

Wolf. Look you, fail not. I cannot wait her recovery—danger surrounds us.

Robbers. [*Advancing.*] Danger!

Wolf. Ay, every eye must be vigilant, every heart resolved—Riber has been stabbed.

Lot. Then Friberg——

Wolf. Has escaped.

Lot. Thank heaven!

Wolf. How?

Lot. Friberg is still reserved for me.

Wolf. Be it so—your firmness shall be proved.

Rav. So—one act of villany is spared you; pursue your fate no farther—desist, be warned in time.

Wolf. Fool! could woman's weakness urge me to retreat, my duty to our band would now make such repentance treachery.

Robbers. Noble captain!

Wolf. Mark you, my comrades: Kelmar has fled; left his house—no doubt for the Chateau Friberg. The suspicions of the Count are upon him. All mistrust of me is banished from his mind, and I have lured him and his companion to the cottage of our lost comrade, Riber.

Lot. How came Claudine to fall into your power?

Wolf. I encountered her alone, as I left Kelmar's cottage. She had been to seek her father; I seized the opportunity, and conveyed her to the secret pass in the forest; her cries caused me to be pursued, and one instant later I had fallen into their hands—by this time they have recovered the path-way to the mill. Spiller shall supply Riber's place—be prepared to meet them at the Flask, and prove yourself——

Lot. The man I am; I swear it.

Wolf. Enough—I am content!

Rav. Content! such guilt as thine can never feel content. Never will thy corroded heart have rest—years of security have made you rash, incautious—wanton in thy cruelty—and you will never rest until your mistaken policy destroys your band.

Wolf. No more of this—her discontent is dangerous. —Spiller! when you are prepared to leave the cavern, make fast the door; Ravina shall remain here confined until our work above is finished.

Lot. I understand——

Wolf. Golotz and the rest—who are wont to cheer our revels with your music, be in waiting at the Flask, as travellers, wandering Savoyards, till the Count and his follower are safe within our toils; the delusion may spare us trouble. I know them resolute and fierce; and, should they once suspect, though our numbers overpower them, the purchase may cost us dear. Away—time presses—Spiller—remember——

Lot. Fear me not—you soon shall know me.

[*Exit Wolf and Robbers up the steps,* L. *in flat—Lothair immediately runs up the steps to the magazine, and places the fusée within, closes the door, and directs it towards the trap by which he first entered the cave,* R. U. E.

Rav. Now, then, hold firm, my heart and hand; one act of vengeance, one dreadful triumph, and I meet henceforth the hatred, the contempt of Wolf, without a sigh.

[In great agitation—she advances to the table, R. U. E., *and, taking a vial from her bosom, pours the contents into a cup, and goes cautiously across to where Claudine has been conducted.*

Rav. As she revives—ere yet her bewildered senses proclaim her situation, she will drink—and——

[Lothair, who has watched the conduct of Ravina, seizes the cup, and casts it away.

Lot. [*Coming down,* L. C.] Hold, mistaken woman! is this your pity for the unfortunate—of your own sex, too?—Are you the advocate of justice and of mercy—who dare condemn the cruelty of Wolf, yet with your own hand would destroy an innocent fellow-creature, broken-hearted, helpless, and forlorn?—Oh, shame! shame!

Rav. (R. C.) And who is he that dares to school me thus?

Lot. Who am I?

Rav. Ay! that talk of justice and of mercy, yet pant to shed the blood of Friberg!

Lot. [*Aside.*] Now, dared I trust her—I must, there is no resource, for they'll be left together. [*To Ravina.*] Ravina—say, what motive urged you to attempt an act that I must believe is hateful to your nature?

Rav. Have I not cause—ample cause?

Lot. I may remove it.

Rav. Can you remove the pangs of jealousy?

Lot. I can—Claudine will never be the bride of Wolf.

Rav. Who can prevent it?

Lot. Her husband.

Rav. Is it possible?

Lot. Be convinced. [*Crossing,* R.] Claudine, Claudine! [*Music.*]

Cla. [*Without,* R. D.] Ha! that voice!

Lot. Claudine!

Cla. [*Entering,* R. D.] 'Tis he! 'tis he! then I am safe! Ah! who are these, and in what dreadful place am I?

Lot. Beloved Claudine, can this disguise conceal me?

Cla. (R.) Lothair! I was not deceived.

[*Falls into his arms.*

Rav. (L.) Lothair!

Lot. (C.) Ay, her affianced husband. Ravina, our

lives are in your power; preserve them and save yourself; one act of glorious repentance, and the blessings
of the surrounding country are yours.   Observe!

    [MUSIC.—*Lothair points to the magazine—shows the
    train to Ravina, and explains his intention—then
    gives a phosphorous bottle, which he shows the pur-
    pose of—she comprehends him—Claudine's action, as-
    tonishment and terror—Lothair opens the trap up the
    stage, R.*

    Rav. Enough, I understand.

    Lot. [*Advancing.*] Be careful, be cautious, I implore
you ;—convey the train where I may distinctly see you
from without the mill; and, above all, let no anxiety of
mind, no fear of failure, urge you to fire the train, till I
give the signal.   Remember, Claudine might be the
victim of such fatal indiscretion.

    Rav. But, Wolf.

Re-enter WOLF, *who hearing his name halts at the back
of the cavern.*

    Lot. Wolf, with his guilty companions, shall fall
despised and execrated. [*Seeing Wolf.*] Ah! [*Aside to
Claudine.*] Remove the train.

    Wolf. Villain!

    [*Wolf levels a pistol at Lothair—Ravina utters an ex-
    clamation of horror—Claudine retreats, and removes
    the train to the foot of the steps.*

    Lot. [*Retreating into R. corner.*] Hold!—you are de-
ceived.

    Wolf. Do you acknowledge it?—But 'tis the last
time.   [*Seizing Lothair by the collar.*

    Lot. One moment.

    Wolf. What further deception?

    Lot. I have used none—hear the facts.

    Wolf. What are they?

    Lot. Hatred to thee—jealousy of the fair Claudine,
urged this woman to attempt her life.

                   [*Points to Claudine.*

    Wolf. Indeed!—for what purpose was that pass dis-
closed?   [*Pointing to the trap, R.*

    Lot. I dared not leave them together.

    Wolf. Vain subterfuge—your threat of destruction
on me and my companions——

    Lot. Was a mere trick, a forgery, a fabrication to

appease her disappointed spirit—induce her to quit the
cave, and leave Claudine in safety.

Wolf. [*Going up to, and closely observing Ravina.*]
Plausible hypocrite, Ravina has no weapon of destruction—how then?   [*Crossing back to Lothair.*

Lot. [*Looking towards Ravina.*] Ah! [*Aside.*] We
are saved. [*Crossing to Ravina, and snatching the vial
which she had retained in her hand, and holding it up to
Wolf.*] Behold, let conviction satisfy your utmost
doubts.

Wolf. [*Looking on the label.*] Poison!—you then are
honest, Wolf unjust—I can doubt no longer. [*Seizes
Ravina by the arm.*] Fiend! descend instantly, in darkness and despair anticipate a dreadful punishment.

[*Music.—Ravina clasps her hands in entreaty, and descends the trap, which is closed violently by Wolf.*

Wolf. Now, Spiller, follow me to the Flask. [*Music.*]
Be sure, make fast yon upper door.

[*He takes his broad miller's hat, for which he had returned—exit up steps, L. in flat., Lothair following,
and looking back significantly at Claudine, who then
advances cautiously, opens the trap, and gives the
train to Ravina—Appropriate Music—Ravina and
Claudine remain up in attitude, the latter watching
Lothair, with uplifted hands.*

SCENE IV.—*The Cottage of Riber.—The sign of the
Flask at the door, L. in the flat.*

Enter COUNT FREDERICK FRIBERG, *and* KARL, R.

Count. This must be the house!

Karl. (R.) Clear as day-light; look, sir, the " Flask!"
Oh, and there stands the mill! I suppose old rough-and-
tough, master Grindoff, will be here presently. Well,
I'm glad we are in the right road at last; for such ins
and outs, and ups and downs, and circumbendi uses in
that forest I never——

Count. (L.) True; we may now obtain guides and
assistance to pursue that ruffian!

Karl. [*Aside.*] Pursue again!—not to save all the she
sex!—flesh and blood can't stand this.

Count. [*Abstracted.*] Yet, after so long an absence,
delay is doubly irksome—could I but see her my heart
doats on!

Karl. Ah! could I but see what my heart doats on.

Count. My sweet Laurette!

Karl. A dish of saur-kraut!

Count. [*Crossing to* R.] Fool!

Karl. (L.) Fool! so I mustn't enjoy a good dinner even in imagination.

Count. (R.) Still complaining!

Karl. How can I help it, sir? I can't live upon air, as you do.

Count. You had plenty last night.

Karl. So I had last Christmas, sir; and what sort of a supper was it, after all?—One apple, two pears, three bunches of sour grapes, and a bowl of milk: one of your forest meals—I can't abide such a cruel cold diet —oh, for a bumper of brandy! but, unfortunately, my digestion keeps pace with my appetite—I'm always hungry.—Oh! for a bumper of brandy!

[*Music heard within the Flask,* L., *in flat.*

Count. Hush!

Karl. What's that? Somebody tickling a guitar into fits; soft music always makes me doleful.

Count. Go into the house—stay; remember, I would be private.

Karl. Private—in a public-house. Oh, I understand, incog: but the miller knows you, sir.

Count. That's no reason all his people should.

Karl. I smoke—they'd be awed by our dignity and importance—poor things, I pity 'em—they are not used to polished society.—Holloa! house! landlord! Mr. Flask.

Enter LOTHAIR, L. D. F.

Karl. Good entertainment here for man and beast, I'm told.

Lot. You are right.

Karl. Well! here's master and I!

Lot. You are welcome. [*Aside.*] I dare not say otherwise; Wolf is on the watch.

[*Wolf appears, watching at a window,* L. F.

Karl. Have you got anything ready?

[*Smacking his lips.*

Lot. Too much, I fear.

Karl. Not a bit, I'll warrant. I'm devilish sharp set.

Lot. Well, you are just in time.

Karl. Pudding-time, I hope! have you got any meat?

Lot. I must ask him. [*Aside, and looking around anxiously.*] Won't your master——

Karl. No! he lives upon love; but don't be alarmed, —I'll make it worth your while; I'm six meals in arrear, and can swallow enough for both of us.

[*Exit Karl, with Lothair, to the Flask,* L. D. F.—*Wolf closes the window.*

Count. Yes, I'm resolved—the necessity for passing the river must by this time have urged the peasantry to re-establish the ferry—delay is needless. I'll away instantly to the Chateau Friberg, and with my own people return to redress the wrongs of my oppressed and suffering tenantry.

Enter KARL, L. D. F.

Count. Well, your news?

Karl. Glorious!—The landlord, Mr. Flask, is a man after my own heart, a fellow of five meals a day.

Count. Psha!—who are the musicians?

Karl. Ill-looking dogs, truly;—Savoyards, I take it; one plays on a thing like a frying-pan, the other turns something that sounds like a young grindstone.

Count. What else?

Karl. As fine an imitation of a shoulder of mutton as ever I clapp'd my eyes on.

Enter KELMAR, *exhausted by haste and fatigue,* R

Count. Kelmar!

Kel. Ah, the Count and his companion!—Thank heaven, I am arrived in time! my master will be saved, though Claudine, my poor unhappy child, is lost. Fly, I beseech you, fly from this spot! Do not question me; this is no time for explanations; one moment longer, and you are betrayed—your lives irrecoverably sacrificed.

Count. Would you again deceive us?

Kel. I have been myself deceived—fatally deceived! let an old man's prayers prevail with you! Leave, oh leave this accursed place, and——.

Enter WOLF, *in his miller's dress,* L. D. F.—*Advances,* C.

Kel. Ah, the miller! then has hope forsaken me.—
Yet one ray, one effort more, and——

Wolf. (c.) Thy treachery is known.

> [*He seizes Kelmar by the collar.*

Kel. (L.) One successful effort more, and death is welcome.

Wolf. Villain !

Kel. Thou art the villain—see—behold!

[*With a violent effort of strength, the old man suddenly turns upon the miller, and tears open his vest, beneath which he appears armed—Wolf, at the same instant, dashes Kelmar from him, who, impelled forward, is caught by the Count—the Count draws his sword—Wolf draws pistols in each hand from his side-pockets and his hat falls off at the same instant—appropriate Music.*

Count. 'Tis he! the same! 'tis Wolf.

Wolf. Spiller !   Golotz !   [*Rushes out,* L.

Karl. Is it Wolf? Damn his pistols? This shall reach him.

> [*Throws down the poniard, and, catching the Count's sword, hastens after Wolf, L.—the report of a pistol is immediately heard, L.*

Exit Count Friberg and Kelmar, L.—At the same moment, GOLOTZ *and another Robber, disguised, followed by* LOTHAIR, *burst from the house,* L. D. F.

Gol. (L.) We are called. Wolf called us !—Ah, they have discovered him.

Lot. 'Tis too late to follow him, he has reached the bridge.

Gol. Then he is safe ; but see, at the foot of the hill, armed men, in the Friberg uniform, press forward to the mill.

Lot. This way,—we must meet them, then ; in, to the subterranean pass ! [*Exit Golotz,* R.] Now, Claudine, thy sufferings shall cease, and thy father's wrongs shall be revenged.   [*Exit,* R.

SCENE V.—*A near View of the Mill,* C., *standing on an elevated Projection—from the foreground a narrow Bridge passes to the rocky Promontory across the Ravine,* R. C.

MUSIC.—*Enter* RAVINA, L. U. E., *ascending the ravine with the fusée, which she places carefully in the crannies of the rock.*

Rav. My toil is over · the train is safe. From this

spot I may receive the signal from Lothair, and, at one blow, the hapless victims of captivity and insult are amply, dreadfully avenged. [*A pistol is fired without,* R. S. E.] Ah, Wolf! [*She retires,* L. S. E.

Enter WOLF, R. S. E., *as pursued, and turning, fires his remaining pistol,* R. S. E., *then hurries across the bridge, which he instantly draws up—*KARL *following,* R. S. E.

Wolf. [*With a shout of great exultation.*] Ha, ha! you strive in vain!

Karl. Cowardly rascal! you'll be caught at last.
[*Shaking his sword at Wolf.*

Wolf. By whom?

Karl. Your only friend, Beelzebub: run as fast as you will, he'll trip up your heels at last.

Wolf. Fool-hardy slave, I have sworn never to descend from this spot alive, unless with liberty.

Karl. Oh, we'll accommodate you; you shall have liberty to ascend from it; the wings of your own mill shall be the gallows, and fly with every rascal of you into the other world.

Wolf. Golotz!—Golotz, I say!
[*Calling towards the mill.*

Enter COUNT FRIBERG, *with* KELMAR *and the Attendants from the Chateau Friberg, in uniform, and armed with sabres,* R.

Count. Wretch! your escape is now impossible. Surrender to the injured laws of your country.

Wolf. Never! the brave band that now await my commands within the mill double your number. Golotz!

Enter GOLOTZ, *from a small door in the Mill,* C.

Wolf. Quick! let my bride appear.
[*Exit Golotz,* C. D. F.

Enter RAVINA, L. S. E.—*Wolf starts.*

Rav. She is here! What would you?

Wolf. Ravina!—Traitress!

Rav. Traitress! What, then, art thou? But I come not here to parley; ere it be too late, make one atonement for thy injuries,—restore this old man's child.

Kel. Does she still live?

Wolf. She does ; but not for thee, or for the youth Lothair.

Rav. Obdurate man ! then do I know my course.

Re-enter LOTHAIR, *conducting* CLAUDINE *from the mill, his cloak still concealing him.*

Cla. Oh, my dear father !

Kel. (R.) My child—Claudine ! Oh, spare, in pity spare her !

Wolf. Now mark me, Count : unless you instantly withdraw your followers, and let my troop pass free, by my hand she dies !

Kel. Oh, mercy !

Count. Hold yet a moment !

Wolf. Withdraw your followers.

Count. Till thou art yielded up to justice, they never shall depart.

Wolf. For that threat, be this your recompense !

Lot. [*Throwing aside his cloak.*] And this my triumph.

[MUSIC.—*Lothair places himself before Claudine, and receives Wolf's attack—the Robber is wounded, staggers back, sounds his bugle, and the Mill is crowded with Banditti—Lothair throws back the bridge, catches Claudine in his arms, upon his release from Wolf, and hurries upon the bridge.*

Lot. [*Crossing the bridge with Claudine in his arms.*] Ravina, fire the train.

Rav. I cannot.

Lot. Nay, then, give me the match !

[*Lothair instantly sets fire to the fusée, the flash of which is seen to run down the side of the rock into the gully under the bridge, from which Ravina has ascended, and the explosion immediately takes place—Kelmar, rushing forward, catches Claudine in his arms.*

DISPOSITION OF THE CHARACTERS AT THE FALL OF THE CURTAIN.

COUNT.   KARL.   KEL.   CLA.   LOT.   RAVINA.
R.]   [L.

THE END.

www.ingramcontent.com/pod-product-compliance
Lightning Source LLC
Chambersburg PA
CBHW081304040426
42452CB00014B/2637